THIS BOOK

BELONGS TO

....

....

With so many books out there to choose from, I want to thank you for choosing this one and taking precious time out of your life to buy and read my work. Readers like you are the reason I take such passion in creating these books.

It is with gratitude and humility that I express how honored I am to become a part of your life and I hope that you take the same pleasure in reading this book as I did in writing it.

Can I ask one small favour? I ask that you write an honest and open review on Amazon of what you thought of the book. This will help other readers make an informed choice on whether to buy this book.

My sincerest thanks.

Table of Contents

SUMMARY

A Brief History of Sewing: Sewing is an ancient craft that has been practiced for thousands of years. The origins of sewing can be traced back to the Paleolithic era, where early humans used bone needles and animal sinew to stitch together animal hides for clothing and shelter. As civilizations developed, so did the techniques and tools used for sewing.

One of the earliest examples of sewing can be found in ancient Egypt, where intricate embroidery and decorative stitching were used to adorn clothing and textiles. The Egyptians also developed the first known sewing machine, a hand-cranked device that used a needle and thread to create intricate patterns.

In ancient Greece and Rome, sewing became an essential skill for both men and women. Tailors and seamstresses were highly respected and sought after for their ability to create garments that were both functional and fashionable. The Romans even had a guild dedicated to sewing, known as the Collegium Sutorium.

During the Middle Ages, sewing continued to be an important craft, particularly in the production of elaborate tapestries and embroidered textiles. The rise of the guild system in Europe led to the establishment of professional sewing guilds, which regulated the trade and ensured high-quality craftsmanship.

The invention of the sewing machine in the 19th century revolutionized the sewing industry. The first practical sewing machine was patented by Elias Howe in 1846, followed by Isaac Singer's improved version in 1851. These machines greatly increased the speed and efficiency of sewing, making it more accessible to the general population.

The Industrial Revolution further transformed the sewing industry, as mass production techniques were introduced. Factories sprung up, employing large numbers of workers to produce clothing and textiles on a massive scale. Sewing machines became a common sight in households, as more and more people began to sew their own clothing.

In the 20th century, sewing continued to evolve with the introduction of new materials and techniques. The development of synthetic fibers, such as nylon and polyester, revolutionized the textile industry, offering new possibilities for sewing. The rise of ready-to-wear clothing also had a significant impact on sewing, as more people began to purchase pre-made garments rather than making their own.

Today, sewing remains a popular hobby and a thriving industry. While the advent of mass production and ready-to-wear clothing has reduced the need for handmade garments, there is still a demand for custom-made clothing and unique, handcrafted items. Sewing machines have become more advanced and computerized, allowing for greater precision and creativity in sewing projects.

The Many Benefits of Sewing: Sewing is a versatile and rewarding hobby that offers numerous benefits to individuals of all ages and skill levels. From creating unique and personalized garments to enhancing mental well-being, sewing has a wide range of advantages that make it a worthwhile pursuit.

One of the primary benefits of sewing is the ability to express creativity and individuality. With sewing, individuals have the freedom to choose fabrics, patterns, and designs that reflect their personal style and taste. This allows for the creation of one-of-a-kind garments and accessories that cannot be found in stores. Whether it's a custom-made dress for a special occasion or a unique quilt for a loved one, sewing provides a creative outlet for self-expression.

In addition to fostering creativity, sewing also promotes problem-solving skills and attention to detail. Sewing requires careful measurement, precise cutting, and accurate stitching, all of which develop a keen eye for detail and the ability to follow instructions. Furthermore, sewing often involves troubleshooting and finding solutions to unexpected challenges, such as fixing a broken needle or adjusting a pattern to fit properly. These problem-solving skills can be applied to various aspects of life, both inside and outside the sewing room.

Moreover, sewing offers a sense of accomplishment and pride. Completing a sewing project, whether it's a simple pillowcase or a complex garment, provides a tangible result that can be admired and appreciated. The satisfaction of seeing a finished product that was created with one's own hands is immensely gratifying and boosts self-confidence. This sense of accomplishment can motivate individuals to take on more challenging projects and continue to improve their sewing skills.

Furthermore, sewing can be a therapeutic and stress-relieving activity. The repetitive and rhythmic nature of sewing can have a calming effect on the mind, similar to meditation. Focusing on the task at hand and the rhythmic motion of the needle and thread can help individuals relax and unwind after a long day. Additionally, sewing allows individuals to disconnect from technology and screens, providing a much-needed break from the digital world and promoting mindfulness.

Sewing also has practical benefits. Being able to sew allows individuals to repair and alter their own clothing, saving money and reducing waste. Instead of discarding a favorite pair of jeans with a small tear, sewing skills enable individuals to mend and extend the life of their garments. Additionally, sewing can be a cost-effective way to create unique and personalized gifts for friends and family, saving money on store-bought items.

Types of Sewing: Hand vs. Machine Sewing: When it comes to sewing, there are two main methods that people can choose from: hand sewing and machine sewing. Each method has its own advantages and disadvantages, and the choice between the two ultimately depends on the individual's preferences and the specific project at hand.

Hand sewing is the traditional method of sewing that has been used for centuries. It involves using a needle and thread to create stitches by hand. Hand sewing allows for more control and precision, as the sewer has direct contact with the fabric and can manipulate the stitches as needed. This method is often preferred for delicate fabrics, intricate designs, and small repairs. Hand sewing also allows for portability, as it can be done anywhere without the need for a sewing machine.

On the other hand, machine sewing involves using a sewing machine to create stitches. This method is much faster and more efficient than hand sewing, making it ideal for larger projects or when time is of the essence. Sewing machines also offer a variety of stitch options and can handle thicker fabrics or multiple layers with ease. Additionally, machine sewing produces more consistent and uniform stitches, which can be important for professional-looking results.

While machine sewing offers speed and efficiency, it does require some initial investment. Sewing machines can be expensive, and there is a learning curve involved in mastering the machine's functions and settings. Machine sewing also requires access to electricity, which may not always be available in certain situations. Furthermore, some people find the noise and mechanical nature of sewing machines to be less enjoyable than the quiet and tactile experience of hand sewing.

Ultimately, the choice between hand sewing and machine sewing depends on the individual's skill level, the specific project requirements, and personal preferences. Some sewers may prefer the control and craftsmanship of hand sewing, while others may opt for the speed and convenience of machine sewing. In many cases, a combination of both methods may be used, with hand sewing for intricate details and machine sewing for larger seams or construction. Regardless of the method chosen, sewing is a versatile and rewarding skill that allows individuals to create beautiful and functional items.

Sewing Machines: Choosing the Right One: When it comes to choosing the right sewing machine, there are several factors to consider. Sewing machines come in a variety of types, brands, and models, each with its own set of features and capabilities. Understanding your sewing needs and preferences is crucial in making an informed decision.

Firstly, you need to determine the type of sewing you will be doing. Are you a beginner looking to learn basic sewing skills, or an experienced seamstress looking for advanced features? There are three main types of sewing machines: mechanical, electronic, and computerized. Mechanical machines are the most basic and affordable option, suitable for simple sewing tasks. Electronic machines offer more features and stitch options, making them ideal for intermediate sewers. Computerized machines are the most advanced, with programmable settings and a wide range of decorative stitches, making them perfect for professional sewers or those who want to explore intricate designs.

Next, consider the brand and model of the sewing machine. Some well-known brands include Singer, Brother, Janome, and Bernina, each offering a range of models to choose from. Researching the reputation and customer reviews of different brands can help you gauge their reliability and performance. Additionally, consider the availability of accessories and replacement parts for the chosen brand and model, as this can affect the long-term usability and maintenance of the machine.

Another important factor to consider is the machine's features and capabilities. Look for features such as adjustable stitch length and width, automatic needle threading, and a variety of presser feet. These features can greatly enhance your sewing experience and allow you to tackle a wider range of projects. Additionally, consider the machine's speed and power. Higher speed machines are ideal for large projects or when time is of the essence, while more powerful machines can handle thicker fabrics and multiple layers with ease.

Furthermore, it is essential to consider your budget. Sewing machines can range in price from affordable entry-level models to high-end professional machines. Determine your budget and prioritize the features that are most important to you. It is worth noting that investing in a quality sewing machine can save you money in the long run, as it will be more durable and reliable.

Lastly, try before you buy. Visit a local sewing machine store or attend a sewing machine demonstration to test out different models. This will give you a hands-on experience and allow you to assess the machine's ease of use and comfort.

Basic Sewing Tools and Their Uses:

Sewing is a skill that has been practiced for centuries, and having the right tools is essential for any sewing project. Whether you are a beginner or an experienced seamstress, understanding the different sewing tools and their uses is crucial for achieving professional-looking results. In this article, we will explore some of the basic sewing tools and delve into their specific functions.

1. Sewing Machine: A sewing machine is a mechanical or computerized device that automates the process of stitching fabric together. It is a fundamental tool for any serious seamstress, as it allows for faster and more precise sewing. Sewing machines come in various types, including mechanical, electronic, and computerized, each offering different features and capabilities.

2. Hand Sewing Needles: Hand sewing needles are essential for any sewing project that requires manual stitching. They come in different sizes and types, such as sharps, betweens, and embroidery needles. Sharps are the most common type and are used for general sewing tasks, while betweens are shorter and thicker, ideal for quilting and heavy fabrics. Embroidery needles have larger eyes to accommodate thicker threads and are used for decorative stitching.

3. Pins: Pins are used to hold fabric pieces together before sewing. They come in various lengths and thicknesses, with the most common being straight pins. These pins have a sharp point on one end and a round head on the other, making them easy to insert and remove. There are also specialized pins, such as quilting pins and ballpoint pins, designed for specific sewing tasks.

4. Seam Ripper: A seam ripper is a small tool used to remove stitches. It has a sharp blade on one end and a pointed tip on the other, allowing for precise cutting and ripping of stitches. Seam rippers are invaluable when correcting mistakes or altering garments, as they enable you to remove stitches without damaging the fabric.

5. Measuring Tape: A measuring tape is an essential tool for accurate measurements. It is flexible and can be easily wrapped around the body or fabric to determine lengths and widths. Measuring tapes come in different lengths, with the most common being 60 inches or 150 centimeters. They are marked with both inches and centimeters, allowing for easy conversion between the two systems.

Selecting Fabrics for Your Projects of Sewing: When it comes to sewing projects, one of the most important decisions you will make is selecting the right fabrics. The fabric you choose can greatly impact the overall look, feel, and durability of your finished project. With so many options available, it can be overwhelming to know where to start. However, by considering a few key factors, you can make an informed decision that will ensure the success of your sewing endeavors.

First and foremost, it is important to consider the purpose of your project. Are you making a garment, a home decor item, or something else entirely? The intended use of your project will dictate the type of fabric you should choose. For example, if you are making a dress, you will want to select a fabric that drapes well and has some stretch to it. On the other hand, if you are making curtains, you will want a fabric that is sturdy and can withstand frequent use and washing.

Next, consider the desired aesthetic of your project. Do you want a fabric that is bold and eye-catching, or something more subtle and understated? The color, pattern, and texture of the fabric you choose can greatly impact the overall look of your finished project. Take into account the existing color scheme and style of the space or outfit you are creating for, and choose a fabric that complements or enhances it.

Another important factor to consider is the level of skill required to work with a particular fabric. Some fabrics, such as silk or chiffon, can be more challenging to sew with due to their delicate nature. If you are a beginner or have limited sewing experience, it may be best to start with fabrics that are easier to work with, such as cotton or polyester blends. As you gain confidence and skill, you can gradually experiment with more complex fabrics.

Durability is also a key consideration when selecting fabrics for sewing projects. Depending on the intended use of your project, you will want to choose a fabric that can withstand regular wear and tear. For example, if you are making a tote bag, you will want a fabric that is sturdy and can hold up to heavy items. Consider the care instructions for the fabric as well, as some may require special handling or dry cleaning.

Lastly, it is important to consider your budget when selecting fabrics. Fabrics can vary greatly in price, so it is important to determine how much you are willing to spend before making a decision.

Notions and Accessories of Sewing: The notions and accessories of sewing refer to the various tools and supplies that are used in the craft of sewing. These items are essential for any sewing project and can greatly enhance the overall sewing experience.

One of the most basic notions of sewing is the sewing needle. Needles come in different sizes and types, such as hand sewing needles and machine needles. Hand sewing needles are used for tasks like hand stitching, embroidery, and attaching buttons, while machine needles are specifically designed for use with sewing machines. Needles are typically made of stainless steel and have a sharp point and an eye for threading the thread.

Another important sewing notion is thread. Thread is used to stitch fabric pieces together and comes in a variety of colors and thicknesses. It is typically made of cotton, polyester, or a blend of both. The choice of thread depends on the type of fabric being sewn and the desired strength and appearance of the stitches.

In addition to needles and thread, pins and pincushions are also essential sewing accessories. Pins are used to hold fabric pieces together before stitching and come in different lengths and thicknesses. They are typically made of stainless steel and have a small round head for easy handling. Pincushions are used to store and organize pins, keeping them within reach while sewing.

Measuring tools are another important aspect of sewing. A tape measure is used to take body measurements and determine the length of fabric needed for a project. It is typically made of flexible material, such as vinyl or fabric, and has measurements marked in inches and centimeters. A ruler or a measuring gauge is used for more precise measurements and to ensure accurate seam allowances.

Cutting tools are also essential for sewing. Scissors are used to cut fabric, thread, and other materials. They come in different sizes and styles, such as dressmaker's shears, embroidery scissors, and pinking shears. Rotary cutters are another cutting tool used in sewing, especially for cutting multiple layers of fabric or making straight lines.

Other sewing notions and accessories include thimbles, which protect the finger while hand sewing; seam rippers, which are used to remove stitches; tailor's chalk or fabric markers, which are used to mark fabric for cutting or sewing; and iron and ironing board, which are used to press fabric and seams for a professional finish.

Overall, the notions and accessories of sewing play a crucial role in the success of any sewing project.

Creating a Functional Sewing Area: Creating a functional sewing area involves careful planning and organization to ensure that all necessary tools and materials are easily accessible and that the space is conducive to productive and enjoyable sewing sessions.

Firstly, it is important to designate a specific area in your home for sewing. This could be a spare room, a corner of a larger room, or even a dedicated sewing table or cabinet. Having a designated space for sewing helps to create a sense of focus and allows you to leave your projects set up without having to constantly pack them away.

Once you have chosen a space, it is important to consider the layout and organization of your sewing area. A key aspect of this is having a sturdy and spacious work surface. This could be a large table or desk, or even a dedicated sewing table with built-in storage. Having enough space to spread out your fabric and patterns, as well as room for your sewing machine and other tools, is essential for efficient and comfortable sewing.

In addition to a work surface, it is important to have adequate storage for your sewing supplies. This could include shelves, drawers, or bins to hold fabric, thread, scissors, and other tools. It is helpful to have these items organized and easily accessible, so consider using clear containers or labeling systems to keep everything in order. Additionally, having a designated spot for each item will help to prevent clutter and make it easier to find what you need when you need it.

Lighting is another important consideration when creating a functional sewing area. Natural light is ideal, so try to position your sewing space near a window if possible. If natural light is not available, invest in good quality task lighting that can be adjusted to suit your needs. Proper lighting is essential for accurate stitching and preventing eye strain during long sewing sessions.

Comfort is also a key factor in creating a functional sewing area. Make sure you have a comfortable chair or stool to sit on while sewing, as well as a footrest if needed. Consider adding cushions or padding to your chair to provide extra support and prevent discomfort during extended periods of sewing.

Finally, don't forget to personalize your sewing area to make it an enjoyable and inspiring space. Hang up artwork or photos that inspire you, or add decorative touches such as curtains or a rug to make the space feel cozy and inviting. Creating a space that reflects your personal style and interests will make sewing even more enjoyable and help to foster creativity.

Organizing Your Sewing Supplies: Organizing your sewing supplies is essential for a smooth and efficient sewing experience. Whether you are a beginner or an experienced seamstress, having a well-organized sewing space will save you time and frustration. In this guide, we will provide you with tips and ideas on how to effectively organize your sewing supplies.

Firstly, it is important to designate a specific area for your sewing supplies. This could be a dedicated room, a corner of a room, or even a portable sewing station. Having a designated space will help you keep all your supplies in one place and prevent them from getting lost or misplaced.

Once you have your sewing space set up, it's time to sort and categorize your supplies. Start by gathering all your sewing tools, such as scissors, measuring tape, pins, and needles. Sort them into separate containers or drawers based on their function. For example, you can have a container for cutting tools, another for measuring tools, and so on. This will make it easier for you to find what you need when you're working on a project.

Next, tackle your collection of threads. Sort them by color and store them in a thread organizer or a thread rack. This will not only make it easier to find the right color thread for your project but also prevent them from tangling or getting lost. Additionally, consider investing in a thread stand to hold your frequently used threads within easy reach.

When it comes to storing fabric, consider using clear plastic bins or storage boxes. This will allow you to see what fabrics you have without having to open each box. Sort your fabrics by type, color, or project, depending on your preference. You can also use fabric bolts or hangers to keep your fabrics neatly organized and easily accessible.

For smaller sewing notions like buttons, zippers, and snaps, use small containers or jars with labels. This will help you quickly locate the specific notion you need without having to rummage through a pile of loose items. You can also use a pegboard or a wall-mounted organizer to hang your containers, making them easily visible and accessible.

In addition to organizing your supplies, it is important to keep your sewing machine and its accessories in order. Store your sewing machine in a protective case or cover it with a dust cover when not in use. Keep all the machine accessories, such as presser feet and bobbins, in a separate container or drawer.

Safety Tips for Sewing: Sewing is a popular hobby and a useful skill to have, but it's important to prioritize safety while engaging in this activity. Whether you're a beginner or an experienced sewer, following safety tips can help prevent accidents and ensure a smooth and enjoyable sewing experience.

First and foremost, it's crucial to have a well-organized and clutter-free sewing area. Keep your workspace clean and tidy, with all tools and materials properly stored. This not only helps prevent accidents but also allows for better focus and concentration while sewing.

When it comes to using sewing machines, always read and follow the manufacturer's instructions. Familiarize yourself with the machine's features, functions, and safety mechanisms. Make sure the machine is in good working condition, with all parts properly installed and maintained. Regularly clean and oil the machine as recommended to ensure smooth operation.

Wearing appropriate clothing is another important safety consideration. Avoid loose-fitting garments or accessories that could get caught in the machine or other sewing equipment. Opt for comfortable and fitted clothing that allows for ease of movement. Additionally, tie back long hair and remove any jewelry that could pose a risk while sewing.

Protecting your eyes is crucial when working with needles, pins, and other sharp objects. Wear safety glasses or goggles to prevent eye injuries from flying debris or accidental pricks. It's also a good idea to have a first aid kit nearby in case of minor injuries.

Always use the right tools for the job. Using dull or inappropriate tools can lead to accidents and damage to your sewing project. Keep your scissors sharp and use them only for fabric cutting. Use proper pins and needles for different types of fabrics and projects. Investing in high-quality tools not only ensures safety but also improves the overall sewing experience.

Take breaks and rest your eyes and hands regularly. Sewing for long periods can strain your eyes and cause hand fatigue. Stretching and taking short breaks can help prevent repetitive strain injuries and maintain your focus and accuracy.

Lastly, be mindful of electrical safety. Ensure that your sewing machine is plugged into a grounded outlet and avoid using extension cords whenever possible. Keep cords away from water and heat sources to prevent electrical hazards.

By following these safety tips, you can enjoy your sewing projects with peace of mind. Remember, safety should always be a priority, and taking the necessary precautions will help you create beautiful and safe sewing creations.

Understanding Patterns and Measurements of Sewing: Understanding Patterns and Measurements of Sewing is a crucial aspect of becoming a skilled and successful seamstress or tailor. Sewing patterns serve as the blueprint for creating garments, and accurate measurements ensure that the finished product fits perfectly.

When it comes to understanding patterns, it is important to familiarize oneself with the various components that make up a pattern. These include the pattern envelope, which contains important information such as the size range, fabric suggestions, and the amount of fabric required. Inside the envelope, you will find the pattern pieces, which are typically printed on tissue paper and need to be carefully cut out. Each pattern piece represents a specific part of the garment, such as the bodice, sleeves, or skirt.

Once the pattern pieces are cut out, they need to be properly laid out on the fabric according to the layout diagram provided in the instructions. This ensures that the fabric is used efficiently and that the pattern pieces are aligned correctly. It is important to pay attention to grainlines, which indicate the direction of the fabric's weave, as this can affect the drape and fit of the garment.

Understanding measurements is equally important in sewing. Taking accurate body measurements is essential for creating garments that fit well. Common measurements include bust, waist, and hip circumference, as well as shoulder width and arm length. These measurements are used to determine the appropriate pattern size to use and to make any necessary adjustments for a custom fit.

In addition to body measurements, understanding how to measure fabric is also crucial. This involves knowing how to calculate the amount of fabric needed based on the pattern's fabric suggestions and the desired garment size. It is important to account for factors such as fabric width, pattern repeat, and any additional fabric needed for matching prints or creating pattern layouts.

Understanding patterns and measurements also involves being able to interpret and follow sewing instructions. Sewing patterns typically come with detailed step-by-step instructions that guide you through the construction process. These instructions may include techniques such as seam allowances, darts, pleats, and closures. It is important to read and understand these instructions before starting a project to ensure a successful outcome.

Overall, understanding patterns and measurements in sewing is essential for creating well-fitting and professionally finished garments. By familiarizing yourself with the components of a pattern, accurately measuring both the body and fabric, and following sewing instructions, you can confidently tackle any sewing project and achieve beautiful results.

Mastering Basic Sewing Techniques: Mastering Basic Sewing Techniques is a comprehensive guide that aims to equip beginners with the necessary skills and knowledge to excel in the art of sewing. Whether you are a complete novice or have some prior experience, this book will take you through the fundamental techniques step by step, ensuring that you develop a strong foundation in sewing.

The book begins by introducing you to the essential tools and materials needed for sewing. From sewing machines to needles, threads, and fabrics, you will learn how to select the right equipment for your projects. Additionally, you will gain insights into different types of fabrics and their properties, enabling you to make informed choices when it comes to selecting the appropriate fabric for your sewing projects.

Once you have familiarized yourself with the tools and materials, the book dives into the core sewing techniques. You will learn how to thread a sewing machine, adjust tension, and make basic stitches such as straight stitch, zigzag stitch, and backstitch. Clear and concise instructions, accompanied by detailed illustrations, will guide you through each step, ensuring that you grasp the techniques effectively.

As you progress through the book, you will be introduced to more advanced sewing techniques. You will learn how to sew darts, pleats, and gathers, allowing you to add shape and dimension to your garments. The book also covers techniques for inserting zippers, buttons, and snaps, enabling you to create professional-looking closures.

In addition to garment construction techniques, the book also covers basic alterations and repairs. You will learn how to hem pants, take in or let out seams, and mend tears and holes. These skills will not only save you money by allowing you to repair your own clothes but also give you the confidence to customize and modify garments to suit your personal style.

Furthermore, the book provides guidance on pattern reading and layout. You will learn how to decipher sewing patterns, understand pattern markings, and lay out pattern pieces on fabric efficiently. This knowledge will empower you to tackle more complex sewing projects and create garments that fit perfectly.

To enhance your learning experience, the book includes a variety of practice projects that allow you to apply the techniques you have learned. From simple tote bags to basic garments like skirts and tops, these projects will help you build confidence and develop your sewing skills.

Mastering Basic Sewing Techniques is not just a book; it is a comprehensive sewing course that will empower you to unleash your creativity and embark on a fulfilling sewing journey. Whether you aspire to create your own wardrobe, make personalized gifts,

COPYRIGHT PAGE

INTRODUCTION

Sewing has so many facets and offers so many possibilities. This book shows exactly step by step in words and pictures how the most important work steps and components are implemented and what needs to be considered. In the following, however, it is first about the sewing basics – to refresh for returnees, as an introduction for beginners and as a small technology comparison for professional seamstresses.

CHAPTER 1

MATERIALS NEEDED FOR SEWING

Here you can find out which aids and tools you need for sewing.

SEWING MACHINE

The most important requirement for making garments is a well-functioning sewing machine. Important for the preparation of the sewing work is the correctly used sewing machine needle. It must match the fabric in its strength. For fine, thin fabrics you choose the thickness 70 or 80, for solid, thick fabrics 90 or 100. For leather, jeans as well as knitted and jersey fabrics, special needles are available in specialist shops.

SCISSORS

You need at least two scissors for tailoring. A larger one for cutting and a small one for cutting the threads.
The scissors should only be used for sewing work and should be sharply ground.

IRON

Modern irons work with steam (= steam iron) and with a temperature control. The correct ironing temperature is set for the fabric in question. Irons with Teflon soles are best suited. Tip: Steam irons should be filled half with distilled water and half with normal water.
TAPE MEASURE

The tape measure is not only used for taking measurements, but also for measuring and remeasurement of the garments. Rulers and angles are needed for recording longer seams and similar work.

MAGNET

It serves as a guide tool to be able to sew the respective seam distances evenly. It is also practical for quickly collecting pins.

CHAPTER 2

SEWING SLEEVES AND SLEEVE SLIT

Here's how to sew a sleeve, work a sleeve slit, and insert the sleeve into the sleeve slit.

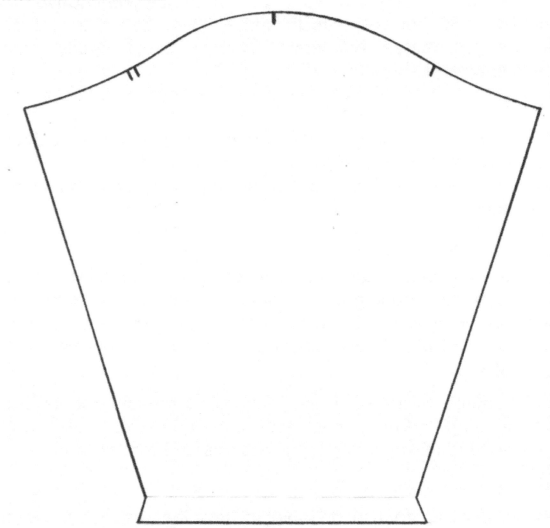

SEWING SLEEVES

Insert the sleeves flat or open. First, close the shoulder seams in the top. In the front and back part as well as in the sleeve there are snaps (front two snaps, back one snap) (Fig. 1) which has to meet. The snap in the middle of the arm ball must hit the shoulder seam (Fig. 1). Place the sleeves and top on the right to the right and close the seam at 1 cm. Make sure that there is no width in the sleeve, or that the width is evenly distributed. Iron the seam allowance into the top. Possibly cut the seam addition of the upper part so that the seam addition fits better, especially if it is solid and non-stretchable fabrics. The seam depending on taste narrow, as well as foot-wide quilt and iron again. Close the sleeve and side seam together on the right to the right and iron it back.

INSERT SLEEVES

Place the sleeves on the right side of the arm cut-out edge, the snaps in the front and back must be congruent with those in the sleeve. The snap in the middle of the arm ball is located on the shoulder seam. If the sleeve is working with rolling width, this must be adhered to between the snaps. If necessary, keep the width in this area with a thread before sewing in. Sew seam and iron seam addition into the top.

SIMPLE SLEEVE SLIT

Cut the sleeve according to the character (Fig. 1). Cut a piping strip 2 cm wide in an oblique thread run. Place the piping strip on the right to the left on the edge of the slit incision of the sleeve (Fig. 2), sew (towards the end of the slit, become narrower!). Iron the piping strip and seam to each other and place the piping on the right side around the seam addition (Fig. 3). Beat the cutting edge of the piping strip 0.5 cm and shred it narrowly from the right (Fig. 4). At the sleeve crossing, place the border inwards.

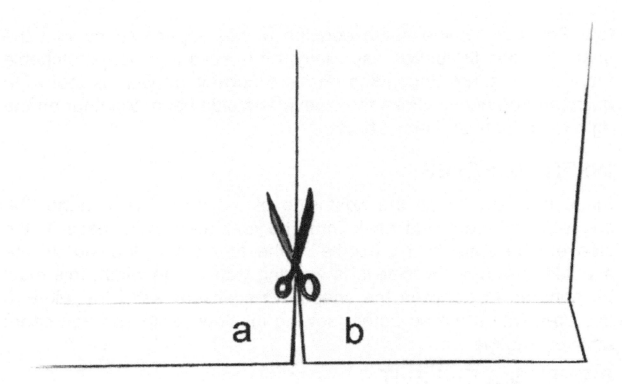

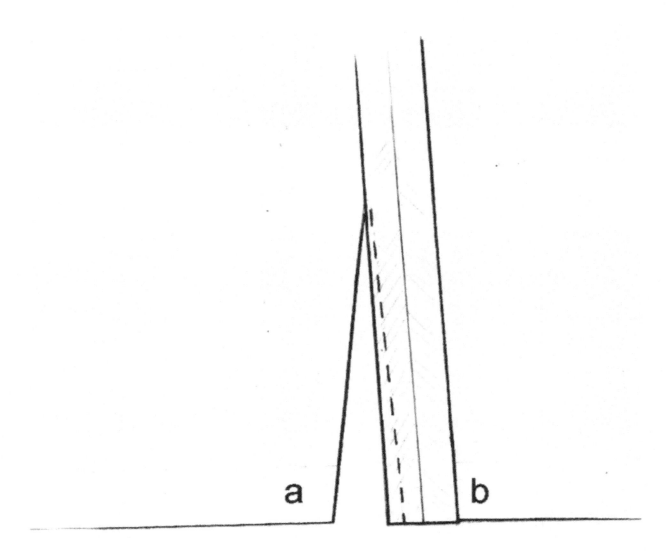

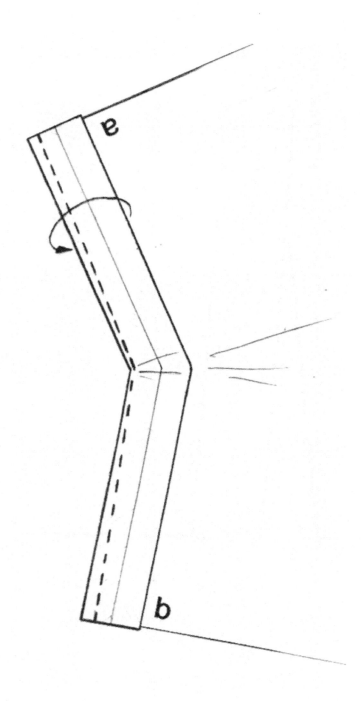

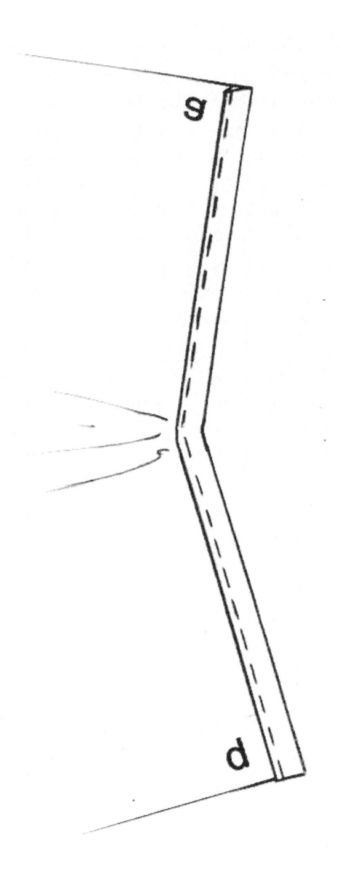

CHAPTER 3

POCKET SEWING

Here you can find out how to sew different pocket variants.

NORMAL ATTACHED POCKET

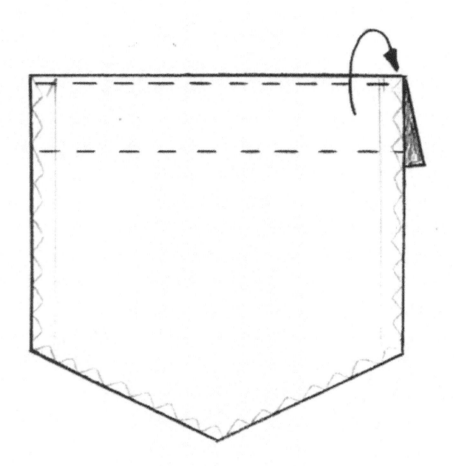

Clean the cut edges. Iron the cut specimen inwards and quilt it at 2 cm.

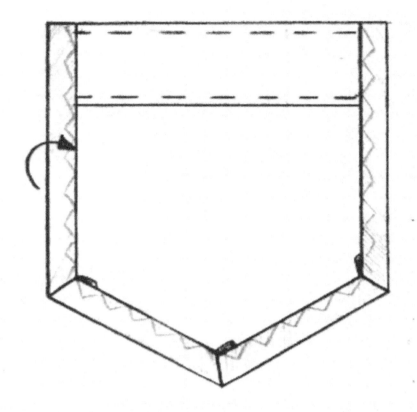

Top edge narrowly quilted.

Cut out the bag (without seam addition) possibly in stronger paper and use it as a pocket template. Iron the cut edges of the bag 1 cm.

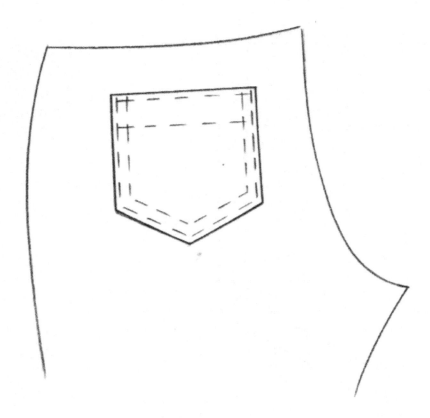

And according to signs narrow as well as foot-wide quilting

POCKET FOR TROUSERS

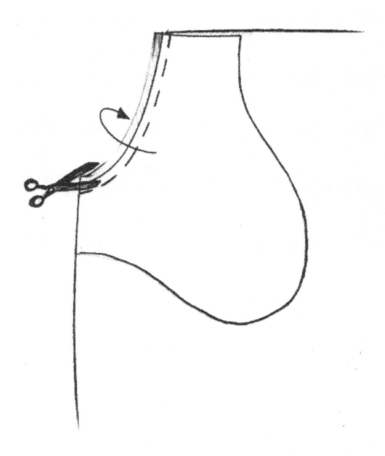

Place front pants and pocket bags right on right and sew (picture left). Cut out the seam allowance to 0.5 cm, iron the pocket bag to the left and quilt narrow and foot-wide. Sew and clean the bag bag with hip part according to the characters on the pocket bag on the right to the right (picture on the right).

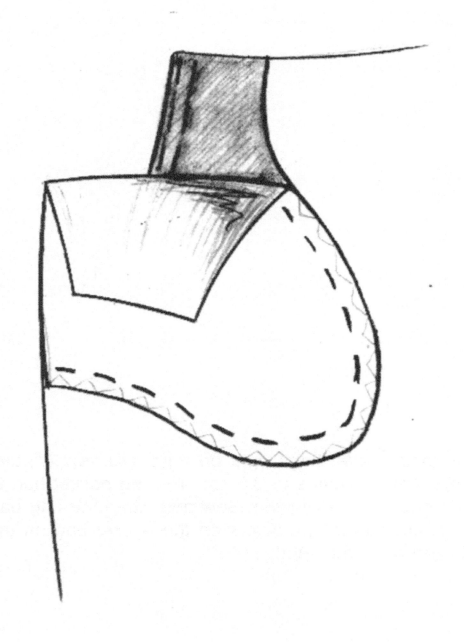

LAST POCKET

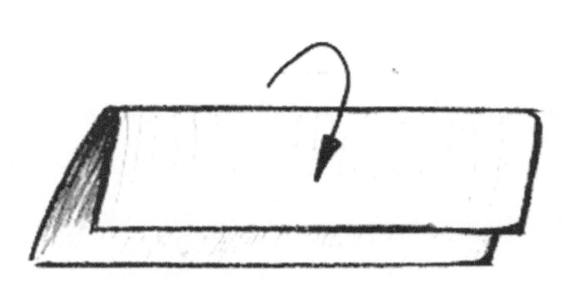

Iron an insert strip on the marked spot from the left. Iron the back pocket bar on the left to the left in the hernia.

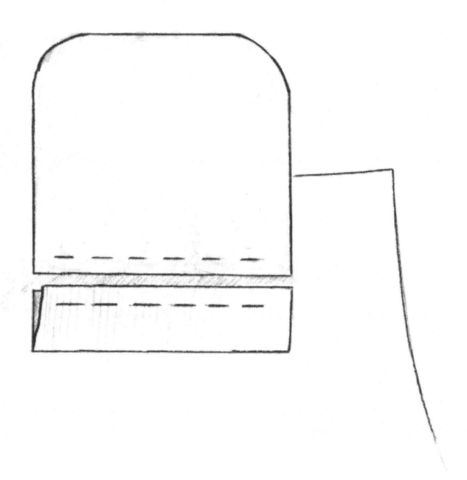

Now attach the bar to the right to the right to the specified place. Bar points down. Attach the upper pocket bag to the right via the bar on the right, the long side points upwards. Sew the seam according to the signs.

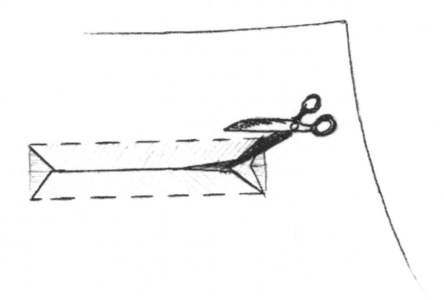

Cut the outer fabric exactly between the seams, cut diagonally into the corners 1 cm in front of the seams.

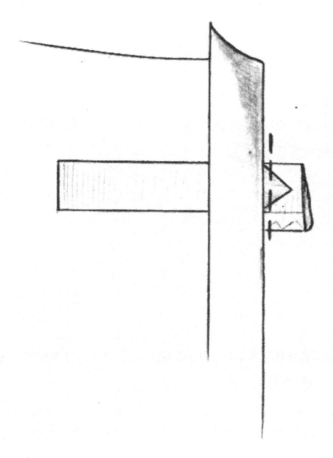

Turn the bag to the left, iron the bar up and the top pocket bag down. Beat the triangles of the outer fabric created by the oblique cutting inwards and tap them onto the strip. The triangles with fixed quilts.

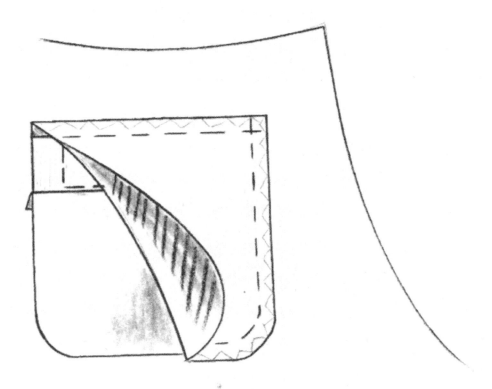

Attach the lower pocket bag to the bar in the middle of the right to the right, the long side points upwards. Stitch the pocket bag from the left exactly on the seam of the strip.

Iron the bag downwards and close the pocket bags to the right to the right and clean the seam allowance

SIDE SEAM POCKETS

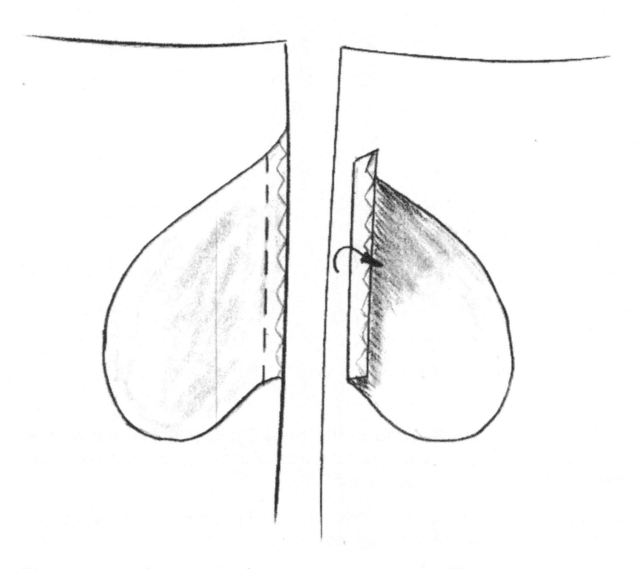

Place on the right on the front or back part, sew (fig. left) and iron the seam addition in the pocket bag. Close the side seam and the pocket bag together (Fig. right) and iron forward.

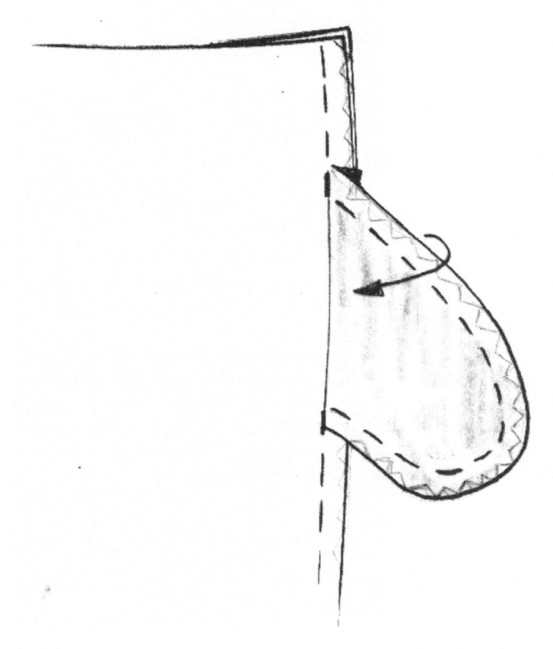

KANGAROO BAG

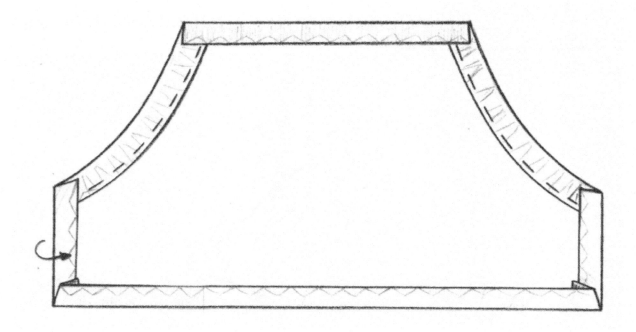

Clean the cut edges. Iron the pocket handle 1.5 cm inwards, stretch the cut edge slightly and quilt narrow-edged. In the case of stretchy materials, iron the insert on the fabric breaks from the left to avoid expansion. Iron the remaining cut edges 1 cm. Put the bag on the front part according to the drawing and tap narrow, as well as foot-width on the front part. Do not quilt the interventions.

CHAPTER 4

ZIPPER SEWING

Here's how to best sew in zippers.

ZIPPERED TROUSER SLIT

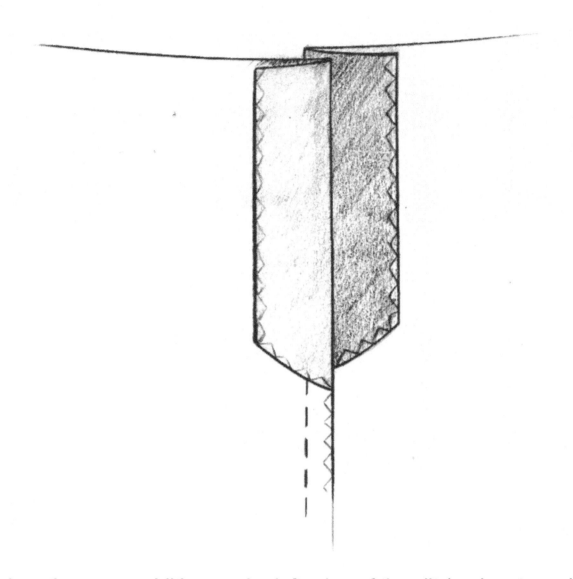

Iron the seam addition on the left edge of the slit (under steer side) 1 cm offset to the front center inwards.

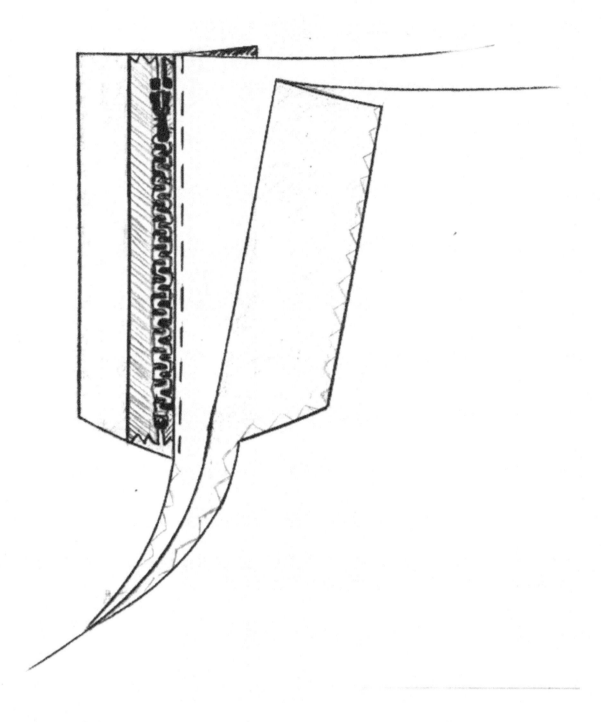

Stitch the zipper underneath, leaving the zipper teeth visible.

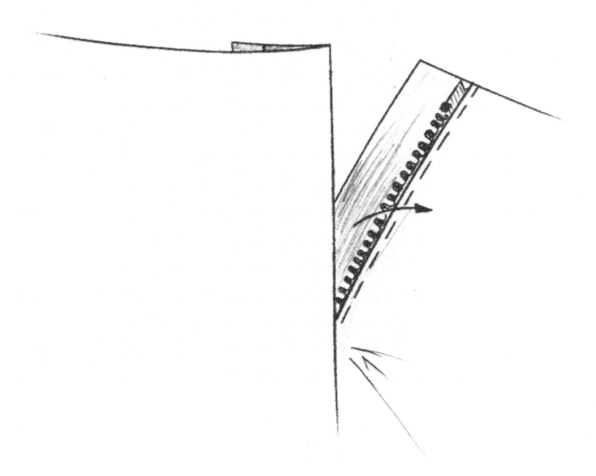

Double the slot entry to the right on the right and topple a narrow side. Turn the under step, clean the open edge and tap under the left slit edge with the zipper, with the closed narrow side at the bottom. Iron the cut receipt inwards on the right edge of the slot (transition side). Insert the slit center to center.

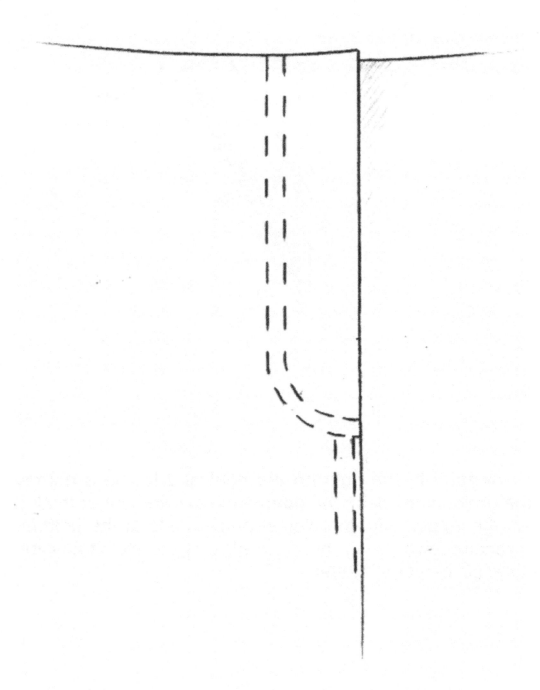

Attach and quilt the loose zipper tape on the inside of the slotted cover, while not grasping the trouser part. The right slit edge in cover width narrow and foot-width quilted, the quilting lines at the lower end of the slot rounded to the seam. Include the slot entry here. Quilt the crotch seam narrow and foot-wide.

SEAM-COVERED ZIPPER

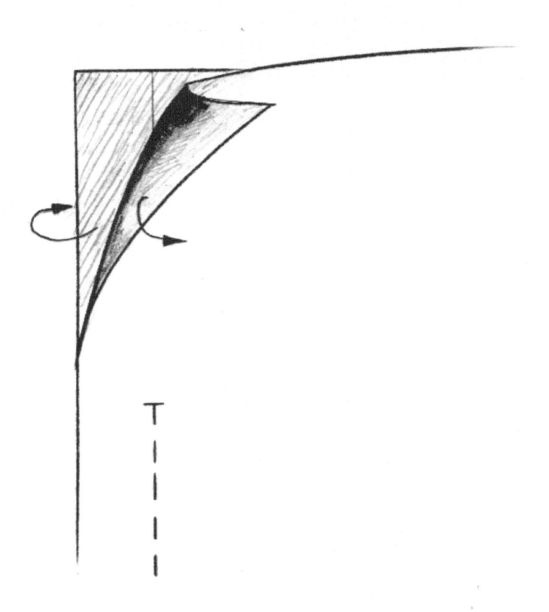

Close the rear center or the side seam to the slot marking and iron the seam addition apart.

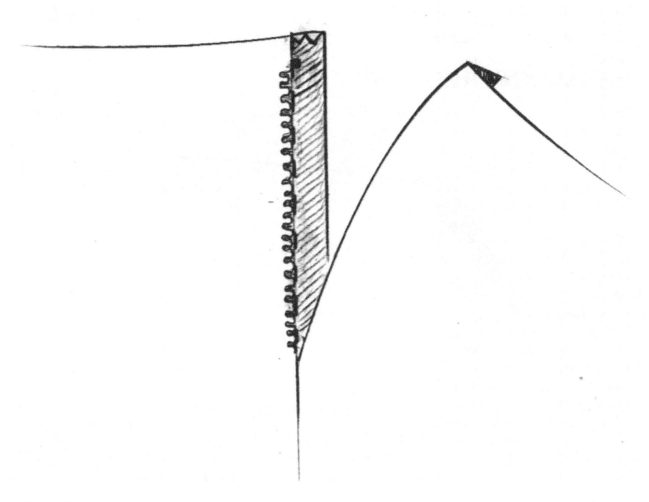

Sew in the seam-covered zipper with the help of a special sewing foot.

These sewing feet are available in specialist shops.

Place the open zipper directly on the edge of the back center and quilt in the zipper shade. Process the other side of the zipper as well. Close the zipper.

JACKET ZIPPER WITH OVER AND UNDERSTEP

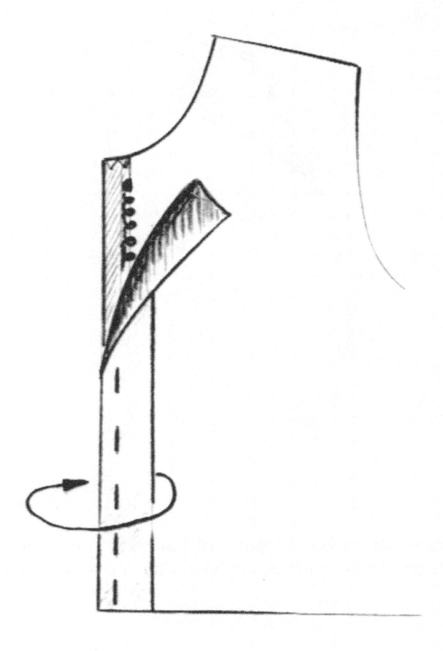

Attach the zipper and the under step to the outside of the front part as described.

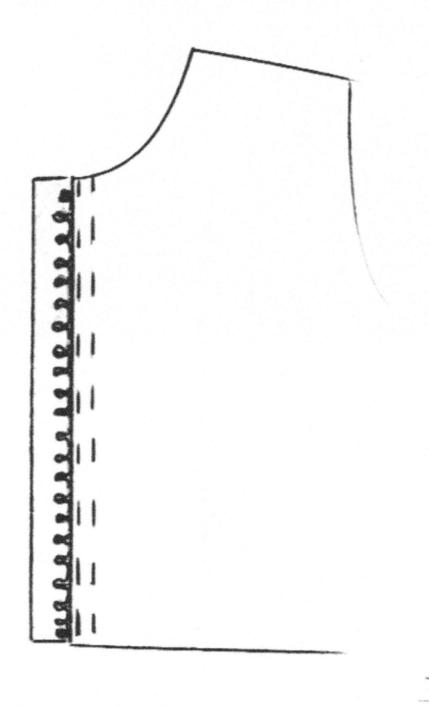

The zipper is located between the front part and the under step and the teeth point to the side seam. Sew the front edge at 0.7 cm.

Iron the under step forward and quilt the front edge narrowly from the right, if necessary also foot-width.

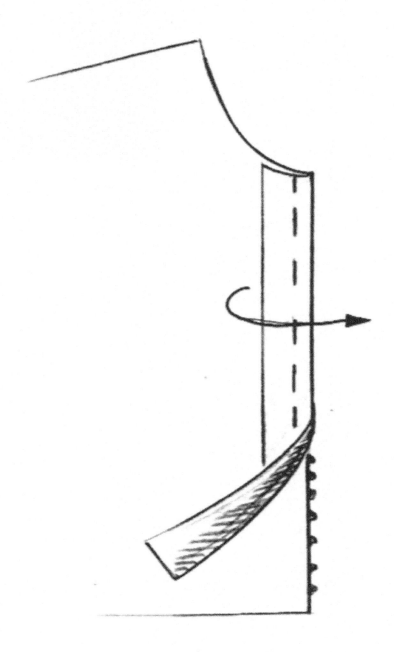

Zipper and the transition according to the signs on the outside of the other front part, the teeth point to the side seam.

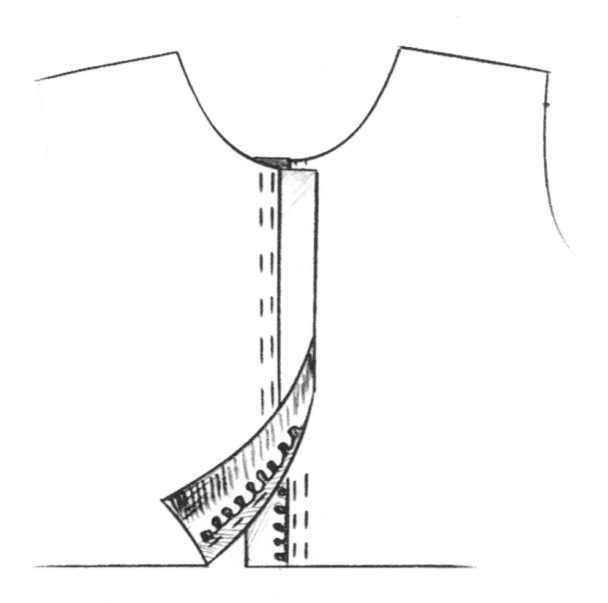

The transition is between the front part and the zipper. Sew the front edge at 0.7 cm. Iron the under step forward and quilt the front edge narrowly from the right, if necessary also foot-width.

ZIPPER IN JACKETS, EDGE TO EDGE, IF NECESSARY WITH RECEIPT

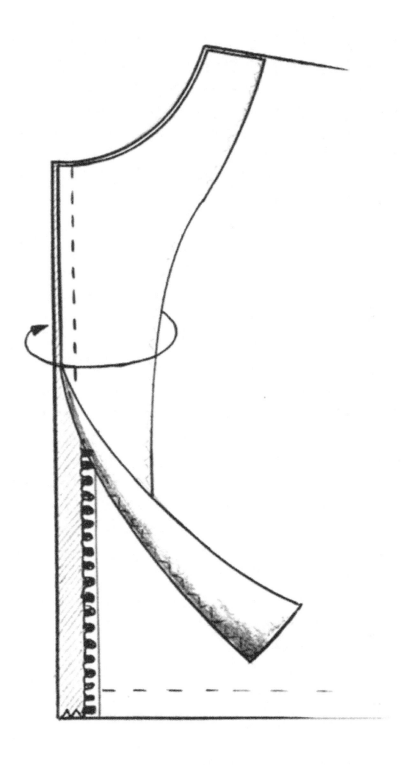

Iron the seam addition of the front edge 1.5 cm inwards and fold out again. Place the zipper with the teeth on the edge of the fracture (teeth point to the side seam). Place the receipt, if available, right to right over the zipper to the front edge and sew everything together with a zippered foot (Fig. left). Turn the zipper or the receipt to the left. The breaking edge lies above the teeth. Also tap the zipper from the left with the zipper foot on the front part, so that from the right a 0.7 cm wide quilting line is created, thereby pushing back the receipt.

Smash the inner cutting edge of the receipt and quilt it on the edge (Fig. right).

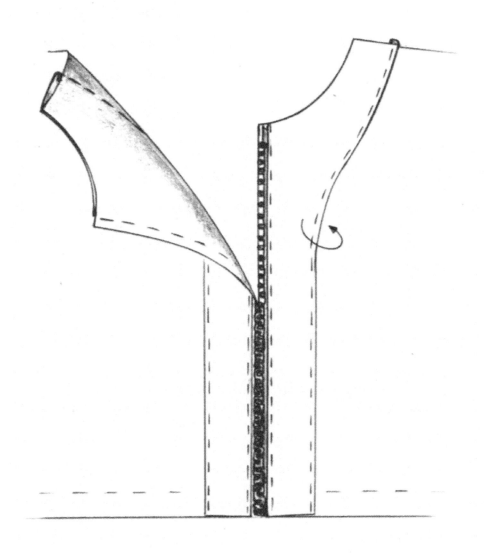

ZIPPER SLOT IN THE FRONT PART

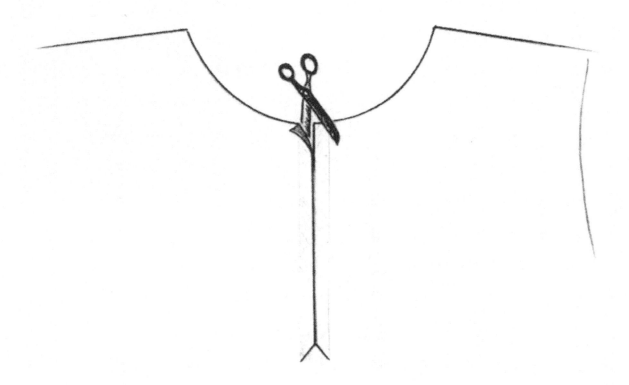

Front center up to 1 cm before the end of the zipper marking and cut diagonally into the corners.

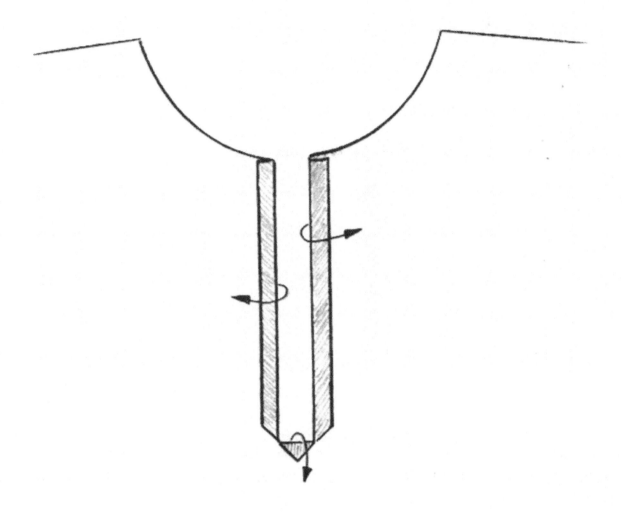

Iron the cut edges 0.5 cm inwards, the small tongue downwards.

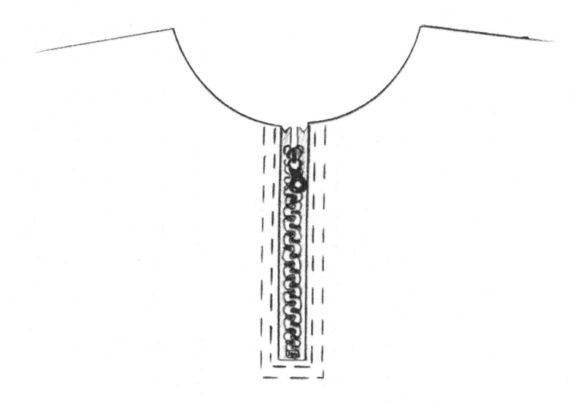

The result is a 1 cm wide slot. Place the zipper in the middle under the slot and pin it tightly. Tap the fabric breakage narrowly, as well as foot-wide on the zipper.

STACKED ZIPPER WITH RECEIPT

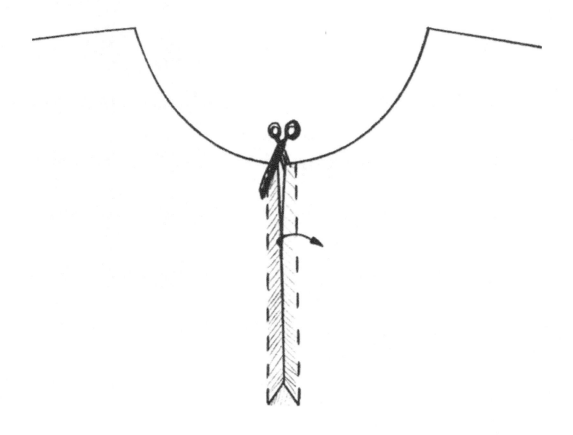

Iron an insert strip on the marked spot in the front center from the left.
Iron the piping strip left to left in the
fracture. Now attach the piping to the right to
the right to the specified location, the break points to the side seam (Fig. left). Sew
the seam and lock the seam ends well.
Cut the outer fabric from the left exactly between
the seams, cut in diagonally 1 cm in front
of the seam ends and
turn the piping to the right (Fig. right).

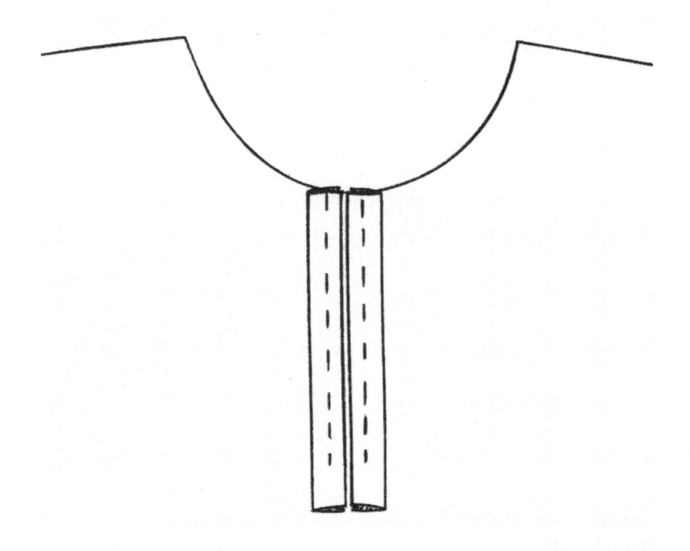

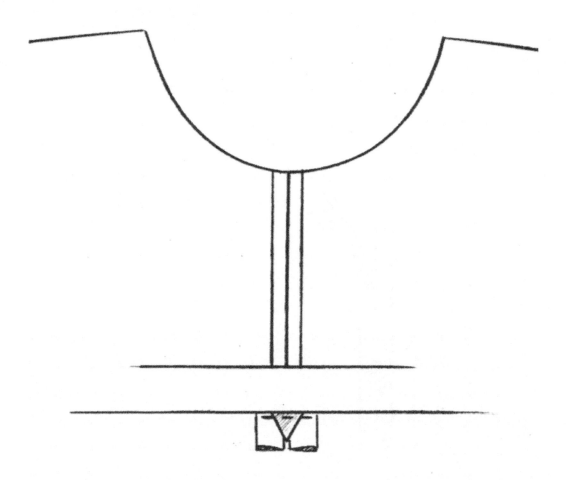

Beat the triangle of the outer fabric created by the oblique cutting inwards and tap onto the piping.

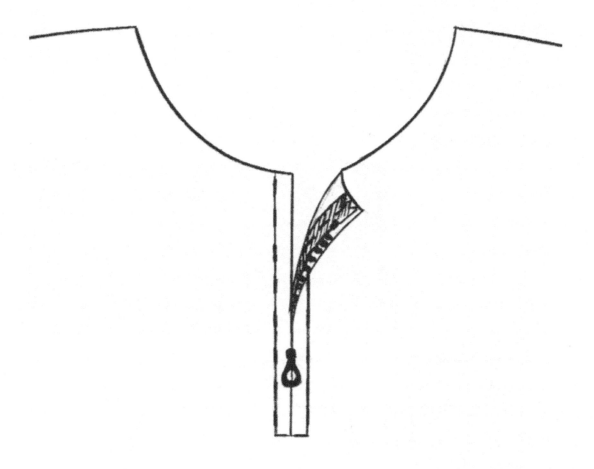

Place the zipper exactly in the middle under the piping, pin and quilt in the shade of the seam.

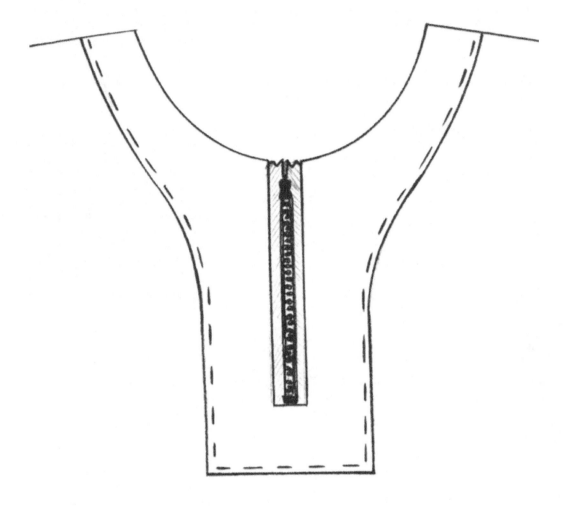

Cut the receipt at an angle just like the front part in the middle and 1 cm in front of the seam end and iron the seam indents and the triangle. Attach the receipt to the zipper tape on the left to the left and attach it by hand. Depending on the model, either iron the remaining cut edges inwards and quilt them up or just clean them.

CHAPTER 5

NECKS, COLLARS AND NECKLINES

Here you will learn how to best sew a collar with a bridge and a stand-up collar.

COLLAR WITH BRIDGE

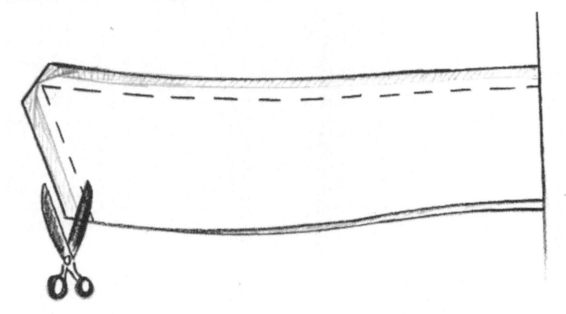

Place the collar right on the right and sew, cut out the seams and cut corners away at an angle.

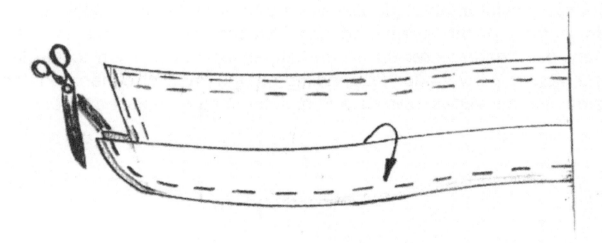

Turn the collar on the right, iron and tap narrow, as well as foot-wide. Place the collar between the two collar bridges in such a way that the collar bars point into the collar.

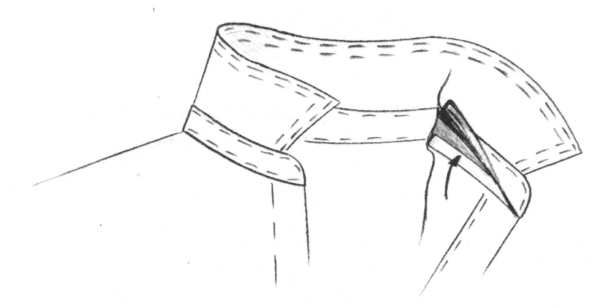

Sewing seam. Cut out the seam addition on the curves tightly. Iron the two collar bridge parts downwards. Sew the inner collar bridge and cut-out right to left (Fig. 3), iron the seam into the collar bridge. Iron the cut edge of the outer collar bridge inwards and attach it to the attachment seam and quilt narrowly. Collar Bridge all around narrowly quilted.

COLLAR

To prepare: close shoulder seams. Sew the stand-up collar to the neckline on the right to the right. Iron the seam allowance into the collar. Turn the other cut edge of the collar 1 cm inwards. Beat the inner seam addition of the stand-up collar inwards and adjust or quilt on the attachment edge.

HEMS AND EDGES

Here you will learn how to best sew different hems and edges.
CARDBOARDING EDGES

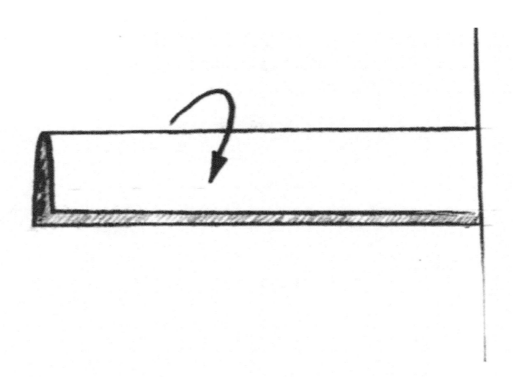

Iron the piping strip left to left to break and clean the cut edge.

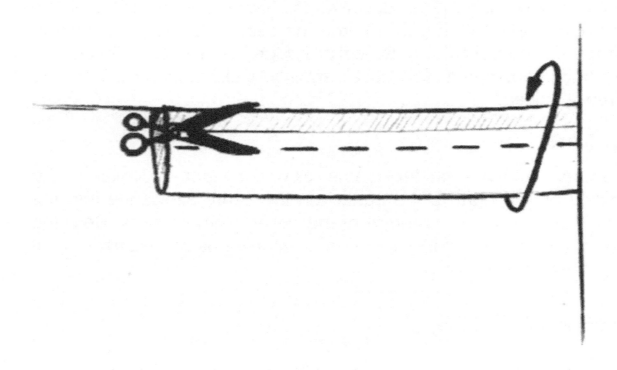

Staple and sew the edges to be pasted and the piping on the right to the right. Make sure that the edge is neither adhered to nor worn out. Cut out the seam allowance and iron the piping inwards.

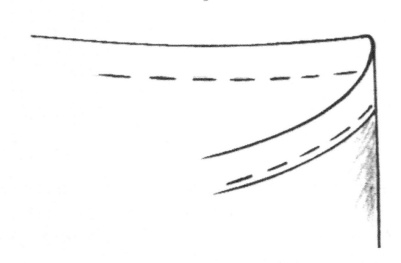

Tap the broken edge narrowly onto the outer fabric from the left.

THE EDGING

Sleeves are often bordered with a small bezel at the end. For an aperture of 1.5 cm, the prepared edging strip must be 5 cm wide. For this purpose, a cardboard template of 3 cm width (double aperture height) and about 30 cm length is cut. The 5cm wide border strip is placed on the ironing board from the right and the cardboard template is placed on the strip in such a way that 1cm seam addition protrudes on each side. Now the addition can be easily ironed around the cardboard strip. Then the template is pulled out of the finished ironed edging strip.

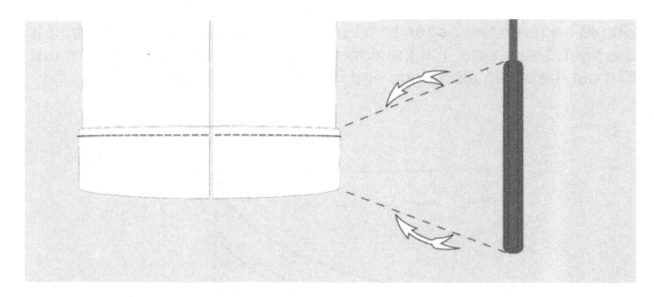

The strip is folded and closed with 1 cm of seam addition to the circle. Then the seam of the strip is placed congruently on the seam of the sleeve. With a few pins, the unfolded edging strip is attached to the edge of the sleeve and the track is sewn in the fold break. The sewn-on strip is now placed to the right around the seam addition. The ironed-in breaking edge is then placed on the attachment seam and fixed with a few pins. The bezel can now be stitched tightly.

TRANSHIPMENT HEMS

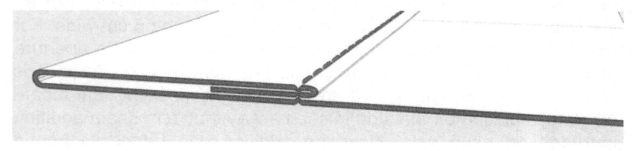

Turnover 1

The cover hem is easy to sew and the most commonly used finish of a garment. For this purpose, the uncleaned fabric is struck twice and this double-beaten route is ironed in. If, for example, the finished hem is to be 2 cm wide, 3 cm must be included as a seam addition for the hem. First, 1cm to the left and then another 2cm to the left is ironed in. The hem is then stitched narrow-edged at the outer folded edge.

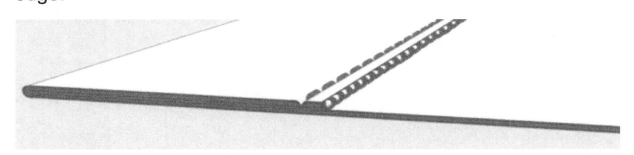

Turnover 2

Another variant of the envelope hem. For this purpose, the edge of the hem cut is first cleaned. Then the hem is ironed 3 cm to the left and quilted on the outer cleaned cutting edge of the hem.

THE ROLLSAUM

The edges of the part to be lined are tightly rolled up and quilted in the same operation. For this purpose, a special roller walnut foot is often used on the sewing machine.

THE BLIND HEM

The blind hem is often used in skirts and dresses. Professionally worked, there is no hem seam on the front of the garment. If you want to sew the hem with the machine, a "blind hem" is needed.

If you want to sew the blind hem by hand, hold the ironed hem so that the over lock seam is exposed at the edge of the hem. This is achieved by slightly bending the fabric at this point. Now, alternating between the outer fabric and the hem, both layers of fabric are sewn together with a sewing needle. Only one tissue thread is absorbed by the outer fabric. At the fabric hem you can take a little more, depending on the type of fabric three to five fabric threads. The thread must not be pulled too tightly. If you have worked well, there is no stitch to be seen from the right side.

LETTER CORNER

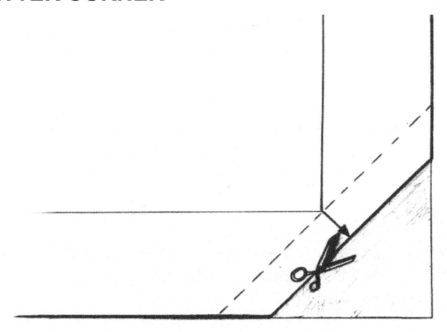

First, cut off the corner at an angle of 45°. 1 cm of seam must remain at the finished corner.

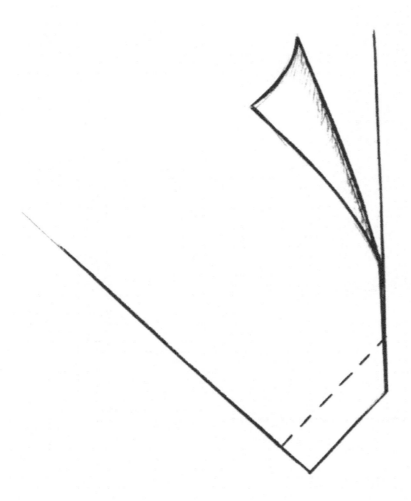

Put the corner to the right on the right...

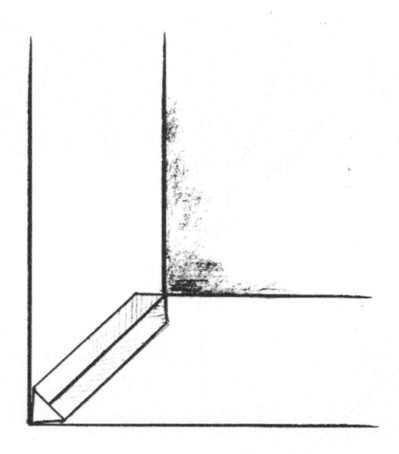

Sew and iron the seam allowance apart.

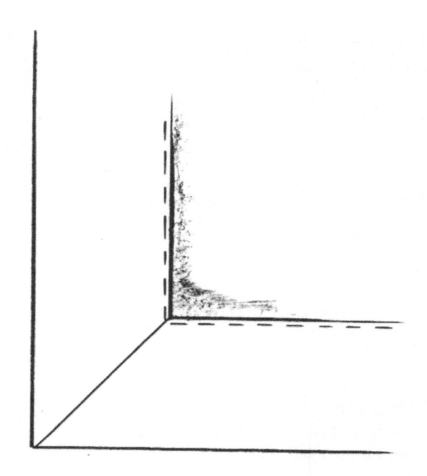

Turn the corner to the left, iron in the hems and quilt up the edge.

FRIZZ

Clean the cut edge. From the cutting edge 0.5 and 0.9 cm wide with large stitch steppe. At the beginning and end of the seam, let the sewing thread hang in long threads and do not lock the ends. By pulling the sub-threads, the fabric can now be compressed.

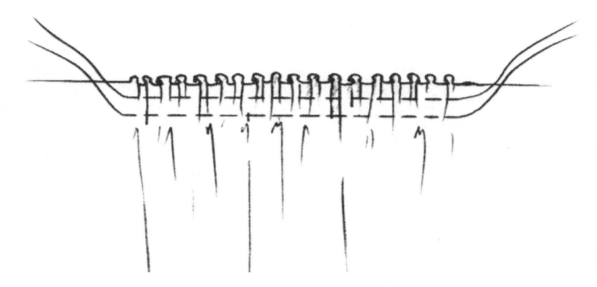

Ripples occur. Contract the fabric to the specified width. If the fabric has the desired width, the seams are knotted and the ripples are evenly distributed over the fabric

TUCK

Here's the best way to sew darts.

In order to adapt a piece of fabric to the contour of the body, it is necessary to sew a dart in various places.

There are different darts.

- Chest darts
- Hip darts
- Waist darts
- Elbow darts

According to the figure, the breast dart is sewn either in a slightly concave or in a straight line. If the body shapes are rounder, the dart is sewn in a concave line. With a slim figure, you sew rather straight darts.

In order to shape a narrow skirt from the hip width to fit the waist width, the hip darts are sewn. Often these are right and left two darts in the front skirt and in the hind skirt. The darts are sewn according to the same principle as the breast darts.

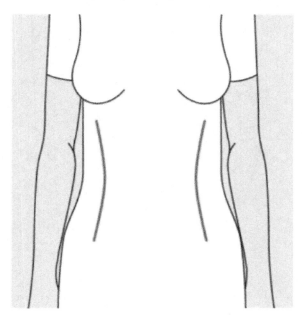

Depending on the figure, the waist dart is sewn in a straight or curved line. For very slim figures you choose the straight variant.

The waist dart often begins a few centimeters below the breast point. It starts with a slightly convex sewn line to the lowest point of the waist. From the waist, one sews in a slightly concave line, which ends in a tip at the level of the hip.

CHAPTER 6

BELT LOOPS

Here's how to best sew belt loops.

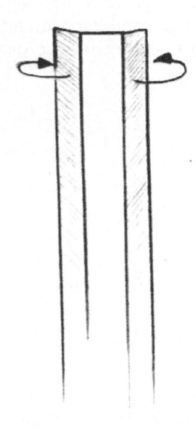

Neaten the two long edges, iron inside out (right side) and topstitch narrowly (left side).

Belt loops to pull through:

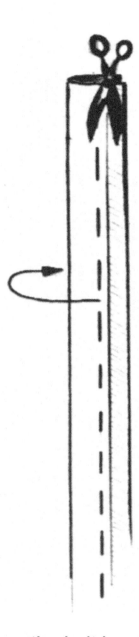

Place the belt loops on the right on the right,

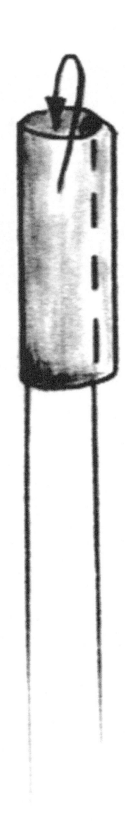

and turn to the right.

Stitch the edges narrowly.

SEAMS

Here you can find out how to best work with additional seams.

RIGHT-LEFT SEAM

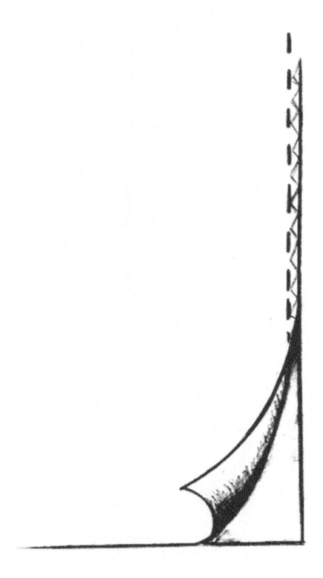

Place the parts to be sewn left on the left, close the seam at 0.3 cm and clean
(right). Turn the sewing material over so that the right sides of the fabric lie on top of each other and sew the
seam at 0.6 cm (left). Iron the seam allowance to one side and quilt it from the right.

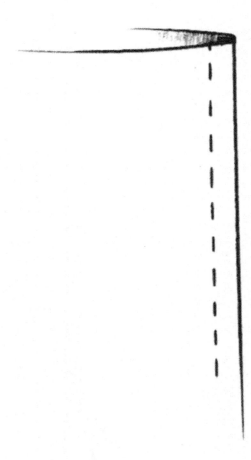

THE END